YOUR KNOWLEDGE HAS VALUE

- We will publish your bachelor's and
  master's thesis, essays and papers

- Your own eBook and book -
  sold worldwide in all relevant shops

- Earn money with each sale

Upload your text at www.GRIN.com
and publish for free

Jens Kaulbars

"Debt is bad" - A refutation

GRIN Verlag

Bibliografische Information der Deutschen Nationalbibliothek:

Die Deutsche Bibliothek verzeichnet diese Publikation in der Deutschen National-
bibliografie; detaillierte bibliografische Daten sind im Internet über http://dnb.d-
nb.de/ abrufbar.

Imprint:

Copyright © 2006 GRIN Verlag GmbH
Druck und Bindung: Books on Demand GmbH, Norderstedt Germany
ISBN: 978-3-656-46843-1

University of Applied Sciences
Bremerhaven

Bremerhaven, 31/10/2006

Jens Kaulbars

„Debt is bad" – A refutation

„Debt is bad" – A refutation

Throughout all the times since humans started to exchange goods for trade, there has been the common opinion that debt is a bad, sometimes even shameful thing to have. Thus it is not astonishing that in Shakespeares' Hamlet Lord Polonius advises his son Laertes: "Neither a borrower nor a lender be" (William Shakespeare, 1598-1602, Act 1 Scene 3), for this clearly expresses the point of view people had and many still adopt. However this would mean a generalization of the term "debt", which cannot be made that easily: "To say that all debt is bad is to say that all debt is alike – which is simply not true" (Tim Cestnick, 2005, p.16).

If one explains debt as "just borrowing money, which gives us greater opportunities and enhances our quality of life" (Lucy Robinson, 2006) it may not be the entire truth, but it sounds far more convenient. Moreover, this quote implies that there is something other than bad debt: good debt.

Now the question occurs, what actually is good debt?
It is the idea of borrowing money to invest, which means using other peoples' money to create wealth. From the view of businesses and private households alike, good debt provides long-term financial payoff.

From the economical point of view, borrowing money means that there is cash available at hand, cash that will be used to buy something or invest in something. This in turn is an injection in the circular flow model and will create profit somewhere. There are three main indicators to look at when differentiating between good and bad debt. The first is the purpose of borrowing, the second the rate of interest and the third is the possibility to deduct interest from tax. This is best explained with some examples, whereat it does not matter if the examples are taken from the business world or from the world of private households, because the principle stays the same.
A common example of debt is the credit card. A credit card is used to buy something and pay for it later, so one could say that it is a form of investment. Alas, usually things bought with credit card are for consumption, therefore perishable and lose value from the very moment they are bought. Consequently financial payoff is not possible. Moreover the interest rate on credit cards is very high and cannot be

deducted from tax. Summarising, according to the three main indicators listed above, credit cards are a way of going into debt, which indeed suits to the statement "debt is bad".

But another good example of debt is a home mortgage. Due to the fact that a home mortgage is like an investment for future life, the value of the object bought from borrowed money gets enhanced. Furthermore the costs of interest rates usually are favourable. Therefore, despite the fact that these interest rates can only be deducted from tax under special circumstances, it is a type of good debt. It is a favourable one, because the value of the object will increase, so it can be seen as an investment which guarantees payoff in future times.

A third example of taking debt is a loan to invest in a business or acquire an asset, where it can be foreseen that it will grow in value. For such an investment interest rates can be quite favourable and a deduction of the interest costs from tax generally is possible, at least in the U.S.A. Therefore borrowing money to invest in something that will increase in worth enables the borrower not only to pay back the credit plus interest, but should also leave him with a personal profit.

Maybe the best example proving that to run into debt, if necessary for a useful investment, is not always a bad thing, is the educational loan. In this case it does not matter if the money is used to support the further education of adults who may already earn their living, or for the education of children or teenagers. The final effect is the same. Applying the scheme used for the examples above, it can be remarked that the interest rates going along with educational credits are usually not very bad. Looking at the most important factor to determine if a debt is bad, some interesting facts can be noticed about the outcome of investing in education. The best way to assess the outcome of such an investment is to look at a report released by the government of the U.S.A. October 26th in 2006. This report implies that the average difference in income per year between adults with bachelor degrees and those with high school diplomas in the U.S.A. is about $23,000. This means that the money borrowed to smooth the way to a bachelor's degree can be paid back in a relatively short time after starting work, because the return on investment ratio is very high.

Summarising it can be said that debt can be of tremendous assistance in building wealth, but the key is to carry the right kind of debt, and not too much of it. In that case debt can be a very good and profitable thing to have.

References

- Cestnick, T. 2005, "The Sraightforward Guide to Maximizing Your LSIF Tax Credits", VenGrowth Asset Management Inc.
- Getlen, L. 2004, "Good debt and bad debt", www.bankrate.com
- Ohlemacher, S. 2006, "College degree worth extra $23,000/year", The Associated Press
- Robinson, L. 2006, "If debt is bad, you're not doing it right", money.scotsman.com Evening News
- Shakespeare, W. 1604, "Hamlet, Prince of Denmark", Second Quarto